There Is a

Story Teller

in My Closet

Story by Gail van Kleeck
Illustrated by
Lesley Avery Gould

*Bringing the Magic of Possibility into
Your Home and Your Life*

There Is a Story Teller in my Closet © Gail van Kleeck, 2015, Published by Abundance Enterprises

First Edition. Printed and bound in the United States of America.

Copyright © 2015 Gail Van Kleeck

ISBN-13: 978-0692577554
ISBN-10: 0692577556

Library of Congress Cataloging in Publication Data

Van Kleeck, Gail
There Is a Story Teller in My Closet

Children's

    There Is a Story Teller in My Closet
    by Gail Van Kleeck

Young Adult

    There Is a Story Teller in My Closet
    by Gail Van Kleeck

Adult

    There Is a Story Teller in My Closet
    by Gail Van Kleeck

Dedicated to my sister,
Lesley, with endless love
and gratitude for her
caring, creative, and
wonder-filled spirit.

Table of Contents

the story teller

There is a story teller who lives in my closet...

For the longest time
I didn't know she was
there.

She says she has been in my closet for years...

Loving me, watching me and wanting to take care of me.

When I didn't know she was there, she felt sad and lonely.

Now when I ask her to come out, she says she feels safer in the closet.

I sit on my bed so we can talk.

When I am pre-occupied,
overwhelmed or too busy
she closes the door almost
completely.

It hurts her to watch me
when I am like that.

When I am more peaceful
and quiet, she opens the
door so she can enjoy being
with me. She has watched
over me for so many years
.... sometimes I think she
knows me better than
I know myself.

Sometimes we laugh together. Sometimes we cry.

She always tells the truth... even if I don't want to hear it.

I like it best when she
tells me stories. She pretends
they are about imaginary
people... I'm not so sure.

I think she changes the
names and places, but the
stories are really about
me.

the boy who
wanted to be good

Once she told me the adventures of a boy who wanted to be good, who tried so hard to please everyone

that he felt tired and confused and angry inside.

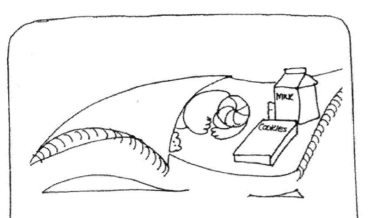

The boy had looked so hard
for the way to be good that
he was exhausted and fell
asleep on the magic rug
in front of the fire.

While he slept, it floated
him safely and gently to
an enchanted garden,

coming to rest right in
front of a friendly old
gardener who seemed to
be expecting him.

"I've looked so hard for the way to be good," the boy said, almost to himself.

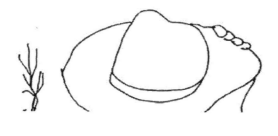

The gardener smiled as though he understood and pointed to a pile of dead branches on the ground beneath a tall pine tree.

"Once," he said, "those branches helped the tree to grow."

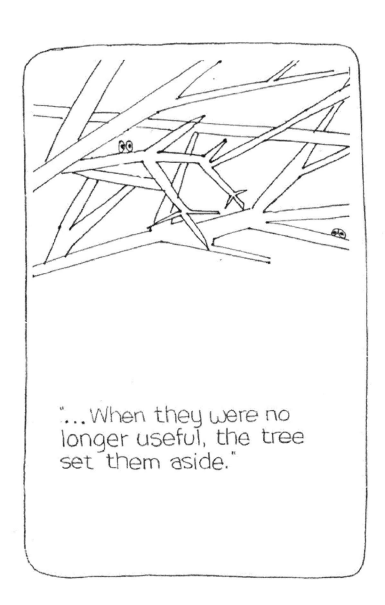

"... When they were no longer useful, the tree set them aside."

"Sometimes," he continued,
"thoughts and ideas are
like old branches and

We need to let go of them
so new ones can grow."

the bird
in the barn

"Perhaps you will find your answer in the barn in the valley," he said,

then without speaking further, the gardener returned to his planting.

The boy could see the
barn from the garden. It
was grey and old. The roof
sagged slightly and its
huge weathered doors
were open wide.

Far above his head he saw
a bird.

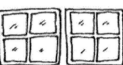

It was flying toward two
small windows high in the
loft... trying frantically to
get out of the barn.

Looking straight ahead, the
bird threw itself against
the glass again and again
... until hurt and exhausted
it fell to the sill.

The boy found a ladder,
climbed up to the loft
and rescued the bird,

carrying it safely out
through the wide open
doors.

the picture

As the boy left the barn, he was so busy thinking about the little bird that he nearly missed seeing the artist who was painting a picture of the pond beside the path.

"Please sir," he said to the artist," will you teach me to make a picture as beautiful as yours?"

"Of course," said the artist.

He gave the boy a canvas
and brushes, then told
him where to draw the
lines and what colors to use.

The boy did as he was told. When he was finished, his picture looked almost exactly like the one on the artist's canvas.

...but the boy wasn't happy. "The picture isn't really mine," he said.

"How would you make it yours," the artist asked?

The boy thought for a moment, then painted a smiling sun in the sky, yellow flowers in the meadow and a small gray duck swimming on the pond.

"Now it is mine," he said
smiling. "My picture is
special. It is not like
anyone else's picture."

the gardener

The boy thanked the artist,
tucked the picture under
his arm and set out on the
path to the garden.

When he arrived, it was
growing dark. The gardener
was cooking supper on a
fire in front of his cottage.
Suddenly the boy realized
how hungry he was.

"I think perhaps there is
more than one way to be
good," he said... passing
his plate for seconds and
remembering the bird in
the barn.

"...And since all of us are special, each of us needs to find our own special way."

The night was quiet and
the boy fell asleep on
the bed the kindly old
gardener had fashioned
from pine boughs.

He dreamed that he and
the gardener were walking
together-down the
mountain path that led
from the garden to the
village in the valley.

different places on the path

The day was bright and warm and very beautiful.

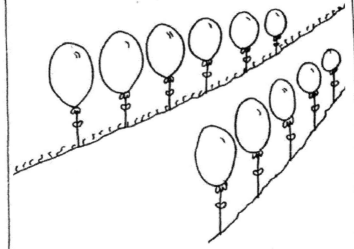

Although the boy had walked the path before, he seemed to notice much more when the gardener was with him.

In the distance, they noticed a man walking towards them.

As they drew nearer the boy could see that the man was hunched over, hurrying along, staring straight ahead. He looked very worried and carried a faded half open, green umbrella.

"What a wonderful day for a walk," the old gardener remarked cheerfully.

"There could be a dreadful storm any moment," the man answered. He pulled his jacket even more tightly around him and hurried up the path.

Laughing for a moment at the man's foolishness, the boy and the gardener walked quietly for a while

They were drawing nearer to the village.

"Sometimes I feel so proud and happy because I think I've learned something," the boy said.

Then I seem to forget and I feel disapointed with myself because it seems I haven't learned anything after all.

The gardener nodded as though he understood and pointed down the path to the church in the valley.

"What do you see." he asked?

"I see the church," replied
the boy. "It is the same
church I see from the
garden on the mountain top,

but it looks different from
different places on the path."
His answer made the
gardener smile.

I will be sad and
lonely without you

The boy caught the old gardener's eye for a moment. "You have been a good friend," he said. "You have taught me many things.

It's almost time for me to go home. I will be sad and lonely without you."

The old man's voice was gentle.

"The more people care about each other, the more they become part of one another," he said.

"At first when they can no longer be together, they feel a sad and empty place deep down inside."

"Then as time passes, they begin to see and hear and feel through the eyes and ears and heart of the person they care about, as well as their own."

"When that happens, they discover that the part of them they thought was sad and empty, is really loving and full after all."

"From now on," the boy said softly, "I will always carry a part of you with me.

It will help me to see and hear and feel with your eyes and ears and heart as well as my own."

The boy looked for a moment at the old man's face.

While the gardener seemed to be smiling, the corners of his eyes glistened softly.

They stopped beneath a
friendly tree and the
gardener spread a picnic
on the grass.

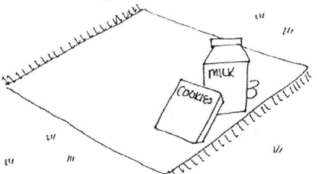

After he had eaten, the boy
fell asleep. He dreamed
he was on the magic carpet
that had brought him to
the enchanted garden...
This time he was going home.

going home

... "How did you like my story," the story teller asked?

"It was very beautiful," I said. "Some parts made me laugh while others made me want to cry."

"Life is like that," she
answered quietly.

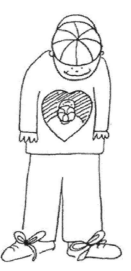

... and although she was
smiling, I thought I
saw tears in her eyes.

The Author and the Illustrator

Gail Van Kleeck and Lesley Avery Gould are sisters. They are the oldest and the youngest daughters in a family of five children who were taught the value of making a difference.

This is the sisters' second collaboration. Lesley helped Gail find a publisher for her first book, *How You See Anything is How You See Everything*, by breathing life into the symbolic, seemingly simple stick-figures she drew at the bottom of each page.

The Author

Gail is an author/interior designer whose positive and empowering attitude can be felt in her stories as well as her books about interior design and moving. She has guided clients in making their homes more comfortable, welcoming and uniquely their own for nearly forty years. The content for Gail's most recent book, *Make Your Move Magically Marvelous*, is drawn from her personal experience as well as the experiences of the countless clients with whom she has worked.

Gail has kept journals and written about the way our focus defines what we see for as long as she can remember. She finds meaning and pleasure from both her writing and her interior design work, because each of them give her the opportunity to make a meaningful difference.

The Illustrator

Lesley Avery Gould left a successful career as an art director for a prominent New York firm to become an underwater videographer. Her love of nature and gift for seeing the beauty and wonder in the world beneath the sea is evident in her work as well as in her personal life.

Examples of Lesley's creativity and the unique perspective of her videography have been featured in New York's Museum of Modern Art and in countless framed photographs that cause viewers to sense something intangible, just beyond the camera's lens. Lesley loves the way symbolism can create richer and deeper meaning. An example of this is the boy in this story, whose shoelaces are untied when he is learning something and tied when what he has learned changes the way he sees.

Books

Make Your Move Magically Marvelous

If you, or someone you know, is planning to move, they will be endlessly grateful for Make Your Move Magically Marvelous. This short and amazingly helpful little book is filled with suggestions and information about where to begin, sorting your belongings, creating storage, packing with unpacking in mind and preparing for the day of your move.

To order, go to:
http://gailvankleeck.org/makeyourmovemagic/

70

There is a Story Teller in My Closet

A little boy discovers a kind and magical story teller in his closet. She tells him stories about imaginary people, but the boy suspects they are really about him. *There* is a *Story Teller in My Closet* is about love and possibility and changing the way we see. It is a wise, tender and thought-provoking story for children of all ages.

To order go to:
http://gailvankleeck.org/simplewisdom

How You See Anything is How You See Everything

Gail Van Kleeck's *How You See Anything Is How You See Everything* is a collection of short, tenderly-woven stories about life's ordinary moments and how what we focus on determines what we see. *How You See Anything is How You See Everything* is an insightful and inspiring little book that is small enough to fit on a bedside table and large enough to change a life.

To order, go to:
http://gailvankleeck.org/howseeanything

Simple Wisdom for Challenging Times

More than just another book of someone else's thoughts, Simple Wisdom for Challenging Times combines a list of A-Z observations with questions that make it a powerful tool for self-exploration and personal growth. Opening and reading just one page a day can make a noticeable and meaningful difference in the way you see and live your life.

To order go to: http://gailvankleeck.org/simplewisdom

CDs

What We Focus On Is What We See

What We Focus on Is What We See is a collection of stories from Gail Van Kleeck's book, *How You See Anything Is How You See Everything* as well as others that are new. The combination of Gail's stories and her calming voice will draw you in and expand your sense of what is possible.

If you listen to this CD while you drive, you are very likely to arrive at your destination feeling more positive and peaceful.

To order, go to: http://gailvankleeck.org/whatwefocuson

Imagine Walking Through
Your New Front Door

This CD about moving is a companion to *Make Your Move Magically Marvelous.* It explores the power of creating a vision for your new home and reinforces some of the book's important themes. Listening to this CD will empower you to make your move with a more positive, confident and open-minded spirit.

To order, go to: http://gailvankleeck.org/imaginewalking

If you email Gail at *gail@homedecoratingfairygodmother.com* and ask to be put on her contact list, you will be notified when her new books and products become available.

Bringing the Magic of Possibility into

Your Home and Your Life

Editing by Barbara Anderson
barbara.anderson@twc.com

Book Design Format and Publishing Assistance
by Connie Dunn
publishwithconnie@gmail.com
http://publishwithconnie.com

Made in the USA
Middletown, DE
27 February 2019